WAR ZONE FAITH

An Army Chaplain's Reflections from Afghanistan

George Tyger

Skinner House Books
Boston

Copyright © 2013 by George Tyger. All rights reserved. Published by Skinner House Books, an imprint of the Unitarian Universalist Association of Congregations, a liberal religious organization with more than 1,000 congregations in the U.S. and Canada, 25 Beacon St., Boston, MA 02108-2800.

www.skinnerhouse.org

Printed in the United States

Cover design by Kathryn Sky-Peck   / Text design by Suzanne Morgan

Front cover photo: U.S. Air Force Capt. David Haltom, a chaplain, provides spiritual guidance to an airman on Balad Air Base, Iraq, March 3, 2009. U.S. Air Force courtesy photo.

print ISBN: 978-1-55896-698-7 / eBook ISBN: 978-1-55896-699-4

6 5 4 3 2 1 / 15 14 13

Library of Congress Cataloging-in-Publication Data

Tyger, George.
  War zone faith : an Army chaplain's reflections from Afghanistan / George Tyger.
      p. cm.
   ISBN 978-1-55896-698-7 (pbk. : alk. paper) – ISBN 978-1-55896-699-4 (ebook) 1. Tyger, George. 2. Afghan War, 2001–Personal narratives, American. 3. Afghan War, 2001–Chaplains. 4. Afghan War, 2001–Religious aspects–Christianity. 5. United States. Army–Chaplains–Biography. 6. Military chaplains–United States–Biography. I. Title.
   DS371.413.T94 2013
   958.104'77–dc23
   [B]
                                                        2012037403

First, for SGT Lex Lewis, CPT Drew Russell, CPT Joshua Lawrence, SPC Michael Roberts, and SPC Christopher Scott—five young men who made the ultimate sacrifice for their nation. May they never be forgotten.

For my wife Jennifer, whom I love more than she will ever know. She has stuck with me through nearly twenty years in ministry, two deployments, and more. Were it not for those family members who hold down the home front, we could never leave for the front lines.

CONTENTS

FOREWORD

———◆———

As a nation, we have been at war for over a decade now. The costs have been immeasurable, for civilians and soldiers alike. Many stories have emerged from Kuwait, Iraq, and Afghanistan—stories of heroic deeds, of endurance, and of brokenness. When Staff Sgt. Robert Bales slaughtered some sixteen Afghan civilians in March 2012, we saw a terrible reminder of what happens when our soldiers lose their moral centers during war. The toxic cocktail of physical injury, traumatic stress, and spiritual challenge can lead some to break down and lose their very humanity.

Into this arena enters the military chaplain corps, armed with nothing but faith, courage, and compassion. These non-combatant officers tend to the soulful needs of our soldiers, and in the process take on multiple roles—preacher, teacher, healer, mourner, leader, listener, wisdom-giver, friend, role model. They are there to help our warriors maintain a moral and spiritual center, that they may never forget their humanity. It is a lot to carry on two mortal shoulders, but carry this weight they do, with grace, grit, and generosity of spirit. Although some have an evangelical agenda, for the most part military chaplains honor their ethical code, which demands that they serve everyone equally in this diverse, pluralist environment. When soldiers' religious traditions restrict the chaplain from performing a particular ritual, their religious needs are accommodated as much as possible—a prayer rug for a Muslim, a quiet place to meditate for a Zen Buddhist.

Chaplain (Captain) George Tyger, one of five Unitarian Universalist chaplains currently serving the U.S. Army (active duty and reserve), represents the best of such ministers to our armed forces, as you will see clearly in the pages before you. George's distance from his wife, Jennifer, and their three children for entire years at a time during deployments has been a sacrifice for him and his family. We, however, are invited to walk alongside George during his most recent deployment to Afghanistan—to smell the odors, feel the tensions and losses, see the dirt-clad children, and experience the respite of a burn-barrel worship service. We get to think with George, pray with George, sip chai and smoke cigars with George, and ponder in our hearts the meaning of it all.

I can see why his soldiers posted George's words of wisdom on the sides of buildings and in the chow hall. He is anything but superior in his tone, admitting his own struggles with judging others, feeling impatient, and at times empty and alone. But George is able to find redemption—mostly in the humanity of others—and he passes those grace notes along. He writes, *Thrown into this broken world, dreadful circumstances sometimes require us to do awful things. When this happens, the life of Christ requires that we turn to each other and see God's people. The life of Christ beckons us to meet our fragmented selves with compassion—standing with, walking with, hoping with, and loving with our fellow human beings.*

I have never served in a war. Yet George's words reach my heart just as they have touched the lives of our soldiers, helping us all find our way home.

Sarah Lammert
Ecclesiastical Endorser for Unitarian Universalist chaplains

INTRODUCTION

———◆———

These reflections were written on my second one-year deployment to Afghanistan. I arrived in Kandahar City, known as the "spiritual home of the Taliban," at the height of "fighting season," June 2011. My job as the squadron chaplain for the 1st Squadron, 10th U.S. Cavalry Regiment was to care for the spiritual and religious well-being of some 1,500 soldiers who would eventually be assigned to our task force, dubbed Combined Task Force Bison. My radio call sign—Bison Archangel— reflected my desire to be on the front line of the battlefield constantly with the soldiers I was called to serve.

Making my home at a mid-sized base near the center of the city, I spent most of my time traveling to the smaller outposts called Police Sub Stations (or PSSs), where U.S. soldiers partnered with Afghan Uniformed Police to bring greater security to the people of the city. But I could not reach everyone. So I began to write "Chaplain's Weekly Briefs" and email them to the Tactical Operations Centers of each PSS. Much to my surprise, I would arrive at PSSs to find my words printed out and displayed in the chow hall, the back door of a latrine, or other places where they would get the most exposure. I received thanks and compliments for words I often penned on the back of scraps of paper while riding in an armored truck. These reflections had to be short to fit easily into the busy lives of deployed soldiers. Yet they had to offer something meaningful to young men and women living their lives in harm's way, far from home. If faith is more about discovering meaning than assenting to particular unprovable statements, this book is truly about frontline faith.

I have done my best to "translate" these reflections so that they make sense to civilians as much as military members, without losing the character of my experiences. Where possible, I have defined military terms or included them in a glossary at the end of the book. One thing I have not done is explain too much about the ideas I've reflected on, or try to tell you what or how you should think or believe. I leave some questions for you to think about, but not necessarily answer. Many of these reflections ask you to make the final choice about your faith. The military has taught me much— perhaps most of all, it has taught me about the power of individual choice to shape the course and character of our lives. As much as military women and men are told what to do on a daily basis, in the end we each make a choice to serve. For most of us, that choice has changed our lives for the better.

What I could not do is find words to fully explain what it is like to be deployed to a combat zone. It is not all shooting, explosions, and fear. Actually, that was a very small part of it. There were long stretches of boredom, hours of work, moments of joy, and some of the most powerful friendships I will ever have. From marathon games of Wiffle Ball on a makeshift field to hoisting casualties into a MEDIVAC bird to memorializing a close friend who never reached the age of twenty five, combat changed me. I believe it was for the better. Yes, there was fear, sadness, death, gore, and many of the things you can imagine war is about, but there was much more than that. While some may not quite understand this, I am glad I deployed and I would not trade that year for anything.

One night, several weeks before going home, I laid awake, thinking of all I had been through. I tried to imagine how this time changed me, or if it had at all. I wrote these lines:

I am an Afghanistan War veteran
I don't want your pity
I served two tours with honor
I've been shot at
Blown up
I put friends into body bags
Seen men die
Sent them home for the last time

According to the popular myth
I should be a
Crazy
Unstable
Angry
PTSD victim
I am none of these
The TV news says you should be careful around me
They say I need help
I will never be the same
Because of what war has done to me

When you look at me
Don't see a caricature
When you hear my story don't sigh and look away
When you think of me don't wish
I had never gone to war

War has not scarred me for life
It has made me more
I am a better man than I was before
I know the value of life more intimately
I know compassion given
And received
I know courage seen
And lived
I know love
For it is love that has kept me alive
Not bombs

Not bullets
Not body armor
These only kept me from dying
Love keeps me living.

Chaplain George Tyger
August 2012
Fort Carson, Colorado

THE ARMY MULLAH

◆

"You *sargin* or commandant?" a young Afghan lieutenant asks as he points to the cross on my chest.

I try to explain what a chaplain is. In the end, he suggests *Army mullah*, and I agree. Not the most accurate description, but the most meaningful for him. *Chaplain* has little meaning for him. *Mullah*, on the other hand, is something he knows and understands. Together with *Army*, we have a term that means something to both of us.

As the night wears on, the Afghan lieutenant and I speak more, with the help of an interpreter, about our very different faiths. We both affirm that the ultimate character of the divine is love. We both believe that the task of religion is to help us live more whole lives. We both participate in a religious community of fellow travelers who give us strength.

Certainly, the words we use are very different. Yet as we do our best to translate our different faith languages into our native tongues, we discover more in common than we thought. We do not try to change each other, only to understand each other.

Whatever religious tradition you call your own, you will probably find religious diversity even within it. We can believe we mean the same things when we use highly charged theological terms like *God*, *Christ*, *Bible*, or *church teachings*. Yet these words convey layers of meaning, not discrete definitions. It is important to remember this and do our own mental translations as we communicate with each other.

That is what I call being religiously multilingual. You need not accept someone else's language as your own. You do not even have to speak another religious language fluently, but you should try to understand enough that you can carry on a meaningful conversation, build mutual understanding, and forge lasting relationships across religious difference. Every such conversation is an opportunity to move the world toward peace.

CALLING

---◆---

The Biblical prophet Isaiah explains his divine calling this way: "I heard the voice of the Lord, saying, 'Whom shall I send, and who will go for us?' And I said, 'Here am I; send me!'"

There was no doubt Isaiah was called. But for most of us, our callings are not so clear. I felt called to one kind of ministry, the kind undertaken in a church, behind a pulpit. Much later, I felt called to another kind—military chaplaincy. This call takes place on the battlefield, at training sites, and beyond. Neither of these callings came with a voice from the sky and flaming seraphim flying above me. I had to tease out a meaningful path from the stuff of my life.

Calling may or may not be associated with a religious element, but I believe it is always about finding meaning. It involves asking the big questions: Who am I? Why am I here? What is my purpose?

Deployment sharpens these questions. In a nation wracked with war, it is easy to wonder whether anything we do can make a sustainable difference. And then we might question whether our sense of meaning depends on our accomplishments. In a mission-focused, results-oriented organization like the military, we may come to believe that our being depends on our doing. It does not.

Job and *mission* are not synonymous with *calling* or *purpose*. My religious tradition teaches that our calling is to be as fully human as possible. Whatever the job we are called to do, we must do it as our most authentic selves. I do not believe that there is a path set out for us ahead of time, but that it is our responsibility to determine who and what we are.

The meaning of whatever job or mission you are currently engaged in is determined by how you choose to do it, how you conduct yourself. This is the calling we make for ourselves day in and day out as we live our lives. It is the calling we all have to be the fully human beings we are created to be.

POSSIBILITIES AND LIMITS

◆

We are on a dismounted patrol to the top of some ancient ruins. A short walk, but the ground is loose and steep. Rocks and dirt slide down as we walk up. The only way to make it up a steep hill while laden with gear is to look ahead but watch where you put your feet.

The same holds true when moving toward any goal in life. Becoming fixated on a goal to the exclusion of the present moment can cause embarrassing and injurious tumbles. But too much attention to the details without looking ahead can cause unnecessary detours. This is the balance of possibilities and limits. The possibilities: reaching the top, hitting on a great idea, realizing a vision of justice and peace, or just getting through the deployment and getting home. The limits: an uncertain course, unstable footing, the dangers of this place, waning physical and emotional stamina. We have hopes, dreams, goals we seek to make real in our lives. We struggle with fear, loneliness, hardship. We must navigate the obstacles while keeping our sights on all that is possible.

We crest the hill and stand atop thousand-year-old ruins. We look out across the city. Children play as well-armed soldiers stroll the streets. In the distance, the earth curves and the horizon falls away. So much possibility. So many limits. Where will we be six months from now? What is possible for our lives? Will we reach our homes safely? Whatever the answers to these questions may be for you, there is only one sure way forward —look ahead, but watch where you put your feet.

THE COURAGE TO ENDURE

One of the things I miss most about home is having a comfortable place to sit. It isn't something most people think about, but over time, it becomes more and more important. Cushioned seats make a big difference. As I travel around, rarely do I find a soft place to sit. Soldiers do the best they can with what they have. However, you can only do so much with plywood and two-by-fours. Most of the discomforts of deployment are small, like plywood seats, but month after month, they add up.

It is easy to pray for things to be better, or different, or just easier. In my experience, these prayers are rarely answered. I don't think prayer works that way anyway. The power of prayer does not lie in its ability to change the world we live in as much as in its potential to change we who live in the world.

Too often, wishing or praying for things to be different leads only to frustration and a downward spiral of negative thoughts and emotions. There are some things that will not change. Confronted with these hard realities, it is better to seek courage to face them than to hope in vain for a miracle.

This courage to endure is more difficult to find than the courage required for a one-time act of heroism. This everyday courage to drive on day in, day out requires more than overcoming fear. It requires us to overcome ourselves.

Maybe you never imagined yourself as courageous. Maybe you see your work as mundane. You are not out kicking down doors, grabbing up bad guys, or stopping the next spectacular attack. Even on a combat deployment, very few of us here are doing any of those things. But that does not mean that what you do does not require a real kind of courage, the kind of courage that gets you out of bed every morning and gives you the power to keep going late into the night.

This courage may not get you a medal. It may go unnoticed. Yet perseverance in spite of all the reasons you could find to give up is something to be proud of. It is this kind of courage that completes the mission and brings us safely home.

EMBRACED BY THE NIGHT

◆

Darkness falls. I sit outside on a clear night looking up at the vast starlit sky. One more day down. How many more to go?

Above, the dome of the sky rounds gracefully into the dark horizon. Beyond that, mystery and wonder. Some things are too vast to fathom. To attempt to understand them ends only in misunderstanding. Other things are finite. They have a beginning. They have an end. Our time here is one of those comprehensible things. Sometimes it can seem like an eternity, but it is not. It had a beginning. It has an end.

One of the great mistakes is to confuse ultimate mystery with finite reality. We want to understand things, so we bring them down to our level. But some things can only be felt in our souls as awe and wonder.

Human beings have tried to name this Truth. We have tried to capture it in words. The great religious traditions each give us a glimpse of it. But none of these words or glimpses can describe the Holy.

We can hold the finite. We must allow the infinite

to hold us. Mistaking the two leads to disappointment when the finite slips from our grasp and we are left reaching for empty air.

For a moment, I look at the stars and long to be home. I long to hold my wife and children in my arms and feel the familiar warmth of their touch. At this moment, even one day more seems too much.

Then I look again. I imagine I am not held captive by the finite days ahead, but embraced by the infinite Truth beyond. I know somehow that the same mystery and wonder that embrace me embrace my family, embrace all. In a real sense, if just for a moment, embraced by God, I am home.

THE BUDDHA'S TOBACCO

I lean back in the chair and exhale a long breath of thick white cigar smoke into the night sky. It rises upward, swirls in a light breeze, and disappears. I think to myself, "Damn this is a good cigar, a good night, and a good place to be for these few moments."

Earlier today, I walked through the local bazaar, where merchants sell over-priced Pakistani knick-knacks and Chinese knock-off designer watches. I held out my arm to one of the kids running around, and he latched onto it and used it like a swing. I lifted him high off the ground. He swung and laughed as I carried him around, just as my own son does at home. It lasted just a moment, but it was a nearly perfect moment in an imperfect place. Moments are all we have — moments of laughter, moments of relaxation, moments to be alive.

It can be hard finding anything good about being in a war zone. It is hot and dirty. It smells bad, there is the constant threat of IEDs or whatever other insane system someone has devised to maim or kill other human beings. Then there is the daily grind of guard duty and details that can feel overwhelming, never ending.

As the sweet smoke disappears, it reminds me that none of this—the smells, the sights, the sounds, the danger, and the grind—none of it is permanent. Maybe the last moment was a bad one. Maybe the next will hold something unwanted. But the present moment can be good if we are present to experience it.

How many moments will you *spend* somewhere you would rather not be? How many moments will you really *live* wherever you are? Those are two different questions. If we spend our moments in regret or worry, if we see the bad in it all, then the moments will grind by one bad day after another and we won't really be living but existing, waiting for "real" life to begin.

But real life is here and it is now. Whatever the conditions may be there is goodness to be found even if it comes in small moments. A moment with a good cigar; a moment playing with a child; a moment with friends. Moment by moment, we live our lives. Like smoke rising into the sky, each moment will fade away into the next and the next and the next. Will you be present for the next moment of your life? It's always up to you.

THE KINGDOM OF GOD

———◆———

There are many understandings of what Jesus called the "Kingdom of God." One is that this Kingdom is possible for all people in the here and now. In the Gospel of Thomas, Jesus' disciples said to him, "When will the kingdom come?" Jesus answered, "It will not come by watching for it. It will not be said, 'Look, here!' or 'Look, there!' Rather, the Father's kingdom is spread out upon the earth, and people don't see it." Waiting patiently will not bring us to God's Kingdom; we must discover it for ourselves. If it is spread out upon the earth, we can find it wherever we are.

It is important to remember the power of Jesus' words, *Kingdom of God*. In the modern world, where gender-inclusive language is the norm, the term *Kingdom* can seem jarring. But in Jesus' time, it was radical. Jesus was proclaiming that the world belongs not to any human king but to God and all God's people. When he said that the Kingdom of God is spread out upon the earth, he was telling them that justice, goodness, peace, and all those things denied them by the elites of the world were not anyone's exclusive possession but the inheritance of all people.

I often need to remind myself of this idea while on deployment. It is easy to get into the habit of seeing only the negative, and there's plenty of it. From witnessing the abject conditions many of the people here must live in, to the constant threat of violence, to the long days, late nights, and time away from home, it is not easy to be here.

Yet the Kingdom of God must be here as well. One of the central teachings of Jesus was that no place and no person is beyond the embrace of God. I cannot deny that there are times when I wonder if there is any good to be found here, but I also know these are the times when I must look even harder.

The question is where I need to look. Usually the answer is that I need to look within myself far more than beyond myself. Generally, it is that which lies within us that most fully blinds us to the Kingdom of God spread out before us. Discovering the Kingdom of God is a choice. We each must choose how we will view the world—as the Kingdom of God or as something fallen and defective.

Despite the violence here, I have witnessed tremendous heroism and compassion. Despite the ugliness here, I have seen beauty in a dusty sunset and in the hopeful eyes of a child. Despite the fear here, I have built lifelong friendships and discovered inner strength

I did not know I had. If I really choose to look, I have seen the Kingdom of God—not just spread out before me but within myself as well.

NAMING GOD

———◆———

Every image, thought, or idea we have of God is a creation of the human mind, not of God. It is easy sometimes to forget this truth. We like to be certain and precise. We are used to language that functions like a directional sign, pointing at the object it represents. When a word does not provide precision, then we dismiss what it represents as nonsense.

In the case of the word *God*, rather than toss out the word, we often try to make it a directional sign. We force it to point to the familiar, certain, and secure elements of our lives so we can avoid the uncertainty of life. In the process of making the word precise, we remove much of its meaning and power. We limit it to only what we can understand or want God to be for us.

Perhaps nowhere is the desire for certainty and precision more pronounced than in a combat zone. We are far from the familiar. Uncertainty surrounds us. In such situations, we crave solid ground on which to stand. It is easy to reach for the one thing that we

16

believe must be certain, unchangeable, immutable—
our idea of God.

The problem is that God then becomes something less than ultimate, a possession, an idol built in our own image. Soon that God becomes our God and no one else's, the God-on-our-side. The next step is to imagine that whatever we do in the name of God is okay. All too soon, God becomes a mere argument we use to justify anything.

The reality of God is so much more than something you or I can build in our minds. The authentic God is necessarily ambiguous and—if we are honest—arrives not as a fact but as a possibility. God exists in the world only in as much as we bring God into the world through our lives.

As soldiers, men and women called to undertake violence in the defense of our nation, the possibility of God is even more important to bring to life, lest we disregard our own consciences and worship nothing more than a parochial God of anger and vengeance who does our bidding.

Possibility awaits us in every moment. God awaits us in every moment. But the possibility of God is not something we can possess. It is not something we can control. It is something we must live in every new moment of our lives as we make the possible become real.

THE ODOR OF LONELINESS

◆

Each morning, I trudge past an overflowing pool of wastewater toward the showers and I think of the words of Henry Rollins, former lead singer of Black Flag: "Loneliness adds beauty to life. It puts a special burn on sunsets and makes night air smell better." I have gotten used to the smell. At night, the smell of the burn pit invades my sleep as it burns away one more day's trash. Walking around the back alleys of Kandahar, I have stepped over stinking piles of human excrement and rotting food. This is a crazy place, so far from the familiar sights and smells of home. It is easy to feel all alone. I'm pretty sure this is not what Henry Rollins had in mind.

Being alone is scary, especially here. Often it's scary because we make it so. The mind wanders to what has been or what might be. We become filled with "if onlys" and "what ifs" until being alone becomes unbearable. At these times, we are most alone because we are not present.

The past is gone. The future is not here yet. This moment is the only one we have to live in. If we are not living in the present, we are not living at all. But we spend much of our time immersed in a private little world of worry and regret.

There is a better way. The Buddha taught this way thousands of years ago in a sutra translated as "A Better Way to Live Alone." He taught, "Never chase after the past or become overly concerned about the future. Everything you need is right here in the present moment. Not tossed about by present or future, that is how you develop heart."

As a military chaplain, I have learned this lesson while crying over the loss of friends and longing to hold tightly to those I love most and never be alone again. Whether deploying to dangerous places, weathering a disappointment, or embarking on a new relationship or career, we all need heart. Where are you right now? Who needs you here in this moment? If you feel alone it is likely because you are caught in the past or chasing the future, rather than finding heart in the present moment, the only moment we are ever really alive.

In time, I will be home with my loved ones again. But right now, I am here. Wherever you are, may you be present there now, with the people who are there with you, so that no one needs to feel alone.

BIRDS HAPPEN

◆

I've received a picture of my youngest son in his new glasses. Also in the picture, perched on his finger, is a bright green cockatiel. I overlook it at first, thinking the picture is taken at a bird-owning friend's house because, when I deployed, I was clear, "No *new pets*." Then I look closer at the photo. The background is just too familiar. "Wait," I think, "that is our house!"

Instructions to the home front are almost always provisional. Understanding this is part of a successful deployment. Conditions "on the ground" change. Things that seemed clear several months ago become more difficult. Not being home, I do not know the specifics of how the bird came to be there. As it turns out, the bird arrived at our home via a friend. It came with all the necessities, all for the sum of $20. A pretty good deal.

I was not part of the bird decision. There are plenty of reasons I could use to justify being angry. After all, I was clear: *No new pets*. Yet there is one overriding reason I cannot be angry: the smile on my son's face.

Your kid's smile justifies many things you never thought you would do or say. Sometimes we must recognize—however irrational it may seem and whatever good reasons to choose otherwise—that that smile is a really good reason to do things you never imagined.

At home, things happen. Choices must be made. We cannot be part of every one of them. Now, when birds happen, I prefer not to ask, "Why?" Instead I ask, "Who did it make smile?" More often than not, that is the most important question—and the best reason for birds, and many other things as well.

WHEN LONELY PRESS LEFT PAW

My son has sent me a "Build-A-Bear." Dressed in the latest digital camouflage ACUs. (Build-A-Bear hasn't yet caught up with multicam.) It came with a note in my eight-year-old's handwriting: "Press left paw for I love you and I miss you." Sure enough, when I press the left paw, my son's voice announces, "I love you and I miss you." I set the bear on my green army field desk.

The bear arrived when I was weary of work and devotion to duty. Unlike the typical day stateside that comes with a beginning (0630) and an end (1700), the days on deployment are not so easily demarcated. There is no "home" to go to, only a cot in a tent just yards from where you work. I walk home every night to a tiny room, seven by nine feet, with a single light. No one is there waiting for me. No one welcomes me at the end of my day. Work continually expands to fill whatever space is available. Nights alone can drag on. Phone calls home are too short and too distant.

At times like this, we all must focus on what truly matters. Many will try to tell you what that is but you must decide for yourself. It's different for each of us. Some say that your meaning and purpose have already been determined. They point to a holy book, creed, or theology. They say what you are meant to be is contained in those particular words and no others. But you must choose to accept the book, adhere to the creed, or subscribe to the theology. No one can choose it for you. There is no way around it.

There are some values honored by all faith traditions: compassion in the face of suffering, love in the face of hatred, hope in the face of fear. But on some long, lonely nights, what really matters is closer to our hearts than any of these eternal values. Right now, what matters for me is a stuffed bear dressed in ACUs and a voice that says, "I love you and I miss you."

INDEPENDENCE DAY, 2011

◆

America's founding fathers believed that human beings were created to be free and that those systems and powers that restrain our freedom also impinge upon our humanity. These are the bedrock of my own beliefs. But as the poet Andre Gide wrote, "To know how to free oneself is nothing; the arduous thing is to know what to do with one's freedom."

In Afghanistan, freedom is always relative to your position and you power. For some, even declaring personal freedom is a risky proposition. For those of us lucky enough to have been born in a free nation, this knowledge should serve as a reminder that freedom is a gift we did not earn. As such, it comes with responsibility. Freedom is not just an idea; it is a tool with which we make ourselves who and what we are.

Your life may not be constrained by concertina wire, high explosives, and IED threats, but each of us has limits placed upon our freedom: jobs we must do, people we have to deal with, where we can afford to live. You can probably name many of your own limits.

As soldiers, we are told where to go, what to do, how and when to do it. In a combat zone, the restrictions on freedom are even greater. From duty hours and uniform standards to the actions of insurgents, many things are out of our control. Some soldiers fight this every step of the way. They despise every order and resent every restriction. I believe that they have failed to clearly see that we are always free to choose how we will respond to those things we cannot control. Will you fight these limits or will you choose you own meaning within them?

Soldiers know how much it sucks to be hot, tired, and dirty, only to be turned around to go on one more mission. We can choose not to care, not to do our best; in short, we can allow circumstances to control who we are and give our freedom away.

On the other hand, all of us can choose to assert our freedom to be something more than a person tossed about by circumstance. We can stand up straight, drive on, and maybe make a real difference. The choice is always ours.

COOLNESS

———◆———

I began my time in the Army as an 11 Bravo, the military occupational specialty known as infantryman or, colloquially, the grunt. When you think "soldier" it is usually the infantryman you have in mind. It was a very long time ago, and I had more than a fourteen-year break in service before I returned to the military as a chaplain. Even so, it took me a little while to recognize that my job was no longer going to involve much of the hooah stuff I did as an infantryman. I would watch the platoons going to ranges, rehearsing combat drills like movement to contact, assaulting a position, or reacting to an ambush—many of the skills I once practiced and wished I could still participate in. However, I soon began to realize that where you want to be is not always where you need to be.

In the Army and in life in general, we have particular missions to accomplish. Sometimes we think that the missions with flash and flourish are the only ones that are important. And by extension, those who perform the missions with flash and flourish are more important than others. It's easy to feel down on ourselves for not doing the "cool" stuff.

Imagine if we each decided only to perform the missions we saw as cool or exciting. Imagine living every day judging your value as a person by what you wish you could be doing instead of who you are right now. Yet this is exactly what we do when we forget that in life and in the military, each of us has a valuable role to fill and an important place in a reality larger than ourselves. In the Army, it is easy to figure out what the right place to be is. Someone will tell you what is expected of you and where you need to be.

In life, however, finding your mission is not as easy. But whatever you may believe about yourself, you have an important place in the world. You are a unique expression of creation. Your job is to figure out how and where the unique and irreplaceable you fits in the world. If you don't decide to be who you are, no one else will be you—and the world will be less for it.

A BIRD IN THE HAND

◆

I sit alone, planning the rest of the day. Last night, I was joking and smoking, in broken Pashto, with the resident contingent of the AUP. I introduced them to the beauty of Dominican tobacco, hand-rolled and perfectly aged. They all seemed to enjoy this symbol of Western democratic values, the fine cigar.

An AUP approached holding a rickety old bird cage, occupied by a rickety old bird. I wasn't sure what to think as he set it in front of me. "Good," he said and gave me a thumbs up.

Not wanting to be rude, I reciprocated the gesture. "Good, nice bird." What else could I say when shown an Afghan's bird?

"Is you bird," He replied. "You keep."

"No," I tried to say, "I can't keep a bird." I stood to return the bird, but he turned and walked away. There I was, flabbergasted, holding my bird in my hand, wondering what to do.

In part, the bird was given in return for the cigars. A gesture of friendship, but even more, an attempt to be known across a deep cultural divide. I didn't want to be rude, but the last thing I needed was a bird, a rickety old one at that. Luckily, another AUP who spoke better English than I speak Pashto returned the bird and conveyed my thankfulness for the gesture. Our new friendship remained intact, bird or no.

We share very little with the Afghans. Our cultures are stunningly different. Our concepts of human meaning and value have dissimilar foundations. Ours is the inherent value of the individual as an individual. Theirs is the meaning the individual gains from relatedness to tribe and clan.

However great our differences, this moment revealed to me an eternal truth: There is something at the core of humanity that makes us the same. We all long for connection. We all desire to be known as ourselves. This human need to be known, even across the widest rifts of culture, may be the one thing with the power to bring lasting peace to our world.

HOPE AND PROFANITY

◆

I have an Afghan friend, a police substation commander, who loves to use profane American slang. I won't repeat the words, but many of them end with the word *bag*. He says them with particular pride and enthusiasm.

When we meet, he says, "Army Mullah, good guy," then points to whoever is next to me and says, "him @?!#-bag." Then he invites us all to sit down for chai and conversation laced with colorful American slang. He says these things with a smile and in friendship so that they take on a different meaning.

At some point in the conversation, the joking turns to serious discussion of the latest incident of violence, the most recent IED or attack. His smile hardens. He leans forward to express the gravity of the subject. Most recently, he leaned in to tell us how one local official, over a period of a few years, had his entire family killed until they finally got to him. While most of his words, except the &$!@#-*bags*, came through an interpreter, I could still understand the grave tone of his voice.

Some things are universal despite language barriers. It is easy to imagine that all of the people in such a violent society accept the violence. My police friend is proof otherwise. His voice betrayed the same sadness, disgust, and anger I felt the day one of my own friends was killed.

Underneath his anger was a deeper yearning for peace. I could not imagine raising my kids in a place like this. I shudder to think of my family having to risk their lives so I could help bring some semblance of peace and security to our homeland. They sacrifice enough having me gone for a year at a time.

My friend has chosen to face the possibility of violence every day because he wants peace. He wants it for the same reasons I do, so our children can grow up without fear. Soon enough, his smile returns, the last cup of chai is finished, and we are all reminded who the ?!%@#-bags are. Some things, like hope and profanity, are universal.

THE COURAGE OF ACCEPTANCE

What does it mean to be yourself? It sounds like a simple question. In the military, we tend to define ourselves by things like name, rank, social security number, blood type, height, weight, PT score. Husband, father, son, daughter, mother, wife — these too are roles that we use to define ourselves. And then there are the opinions of others. Sadly, the negative judgments of others are often more powerful than the positive self-definitions we'd like to claim. Who are you without any of these labels and criticisms?

Paul Tillich said, "The courage to be is the courage to accept oneself, in spite of being unacceptable." Made in the image of God, endowed with inherent worth and dignity, we are bombarded by messages that we are other than this and even less than this. We are told we must be something other than ourselves to be accepted (sometimes this is even called salvation!). Our identities are squeezed into narrow categories. Too often, these messages sink into our souls and we start believing they are true.

There is another message out there, taught by great religious prophets and teachers throughout history. For me, it is exemplified in the life and teaching of Jesus, but it is not exclusive to the Christian faith. That message is simply this: "You are accepted." Despite your flaws and brokenness, you are accepted just as you are. There is nothing you need to do, or believe, or say to earn this universal, unconditional acceptance. But to really believe this in your bones, you need to find the courage to be.

You may ask, "The courage to be what?" The answer is startlingly uncomplicated. You need the courage to be, just to be. Not to be this "thing" or that "thing," not to be any "thing" at all, but just to be, just as you are, accepted by God and yourself as a being of worth. Start with this and you will learn exactly who you are.

LIVING WATER

◆

In the story of the woman at the well (John 4:3–42), Jesus sits with a Samaritan woman, drinks water with her, and offers her what he calls living water. Many cast the Samaritan woman as a woman without morals and say this is a story about sin and the need for repentance. But if you read the story carefully, there is nothing there to support this view and plenty to understand it as a story of Jesus' unconditional acceptance of those others call unacceptable.

As a woman, a Samaritan, and a divorcee, she is a triply unacceptable outcast. Yet Jesus doesn't reject her. The religious and cultural expectations of the time make such a meeting, if not forbidden, then unseemly and dangerous.

In effect, Jesus tells her, "All that stuff about who is in and who is out, about the Samaritans and the Jews, about the clean and the unclean, that is all old news. There is a better way, a new way, and it is not about words like *ritual*, *creed*, or *belief*; it is about life, real life, here and now. It is about how we choose to care for each other. That's what matters. That's the living water God offers to all humanity."

How will we offer living water to each other? Who among us is in need of a cool drink of acceptance? When your buddy gets hot, tired, worn out, and beat down, will you be the one to offer her or him a drink: a word of encouragement, a hand up, a shoulder to lean on?

There are too many things that make us feel like unacceptable outcasts in a combat zone—the barking platoon sergeant, the dirty looks from those we are here to help, the powerful loneliness we cannot hide from— all can make us feel as though we are less than we are. In this place, we must be the bearers of living water for each other. It is up to each of us to see beyond the things that beat us down and keep us apart as we offer the living water of understanding, compassion, and love to our brothers and sisters in need.

NO GREATER LOVE

◆

In the Gospel of John, it is written, "No one has greater love than this, to lay down one's life for one's friends." I thought a lot about that as I tried to make sense of the deaths of two more friends. We must all make sense of such things. Death, whether in combat or in the normal course of life, will touch us all. When it does, we must try to figure out where it all fits in our living. I do not personally believe in a deity that has a cosmic purpose. I believe that finding meaning and discovering purpose in the stuff of living is the purview of living, breathing human beings. Even if you believe that God has a purpose for everything or that you and I make meaning out of the triumph and tragedy of life, your belief is a choice you make.

We in the military have dedicated our lives to many high ideals. Freedom, honor, loyalty, and duty define the American way of life. We place ourselves in harm's way to defend these ideals so that those at home can sleep safe each night. When we lose friends, an emptiness remains which even the highest ideals cannot fill. The cost of those ideals is the struggle to find meaning in these losses.

As I wander around camp this week, these things weigh heavy on my heart. I sit and talk late into the night with friends and soon-to-be-friends. I simply do not want to be alone. I find those who, unknown to them, just by being here, offer the healing and hope I so need. How do they do this? I wish I had an answer. I still have the vision of death in my mind and the smell of blood in my nose. I share a cigar with a young private who tells me about deer hunting in West Virginia. Another tells me about his four-wheeler. There is no magic in their words. They don't even know what I am going through. It is just their presence that matters. Out of this wandering, meaning begins to emerge. Out of this wandering, the emptiness begins to be filled.

Through the power of friendship, we are given a great gift. Beyond the lofty ideals, beneath the noble causes, when all else is stripped away, we are here for each other. When things become difficult, even tragic, we need to know there are friends we can turn to and rely on.

A place of emptiness will always remain for friends I have lost. Yet through and because of this emptiness, I find that I have more friends than I realized. More people care than I have imagined. Allow me to be so bold as to change the words of John: "No one has greater love than this, to be there for one's friends when they need him most." Just being there is sometimes the greatest love in the most difficult times.

WHAT'S IN A NAME?

◆

Meister Eckhart, a twelfth-century Christian mystic once wrote, "If one knows anything of God and affixes any name to it that is not God." We cannot avoid naming God. The very nature of human language requires it. The cross, the Bible, our creeds, even the word *God*—these are all symbols that, in some sense, name God. They are not the reality, but they help us express in rational terms a truth that goes beyond reason. Buddhists have a saying: "Never mistake the finger pointing at the moon for the moon itself." Christian teachings call this mistake idolatry.

I have come to believe mistaking the finger for the moon is behind much of the violence and injustice we see in our world. By claiming one symbol as the only legitimate understanding of God, we make God our possession. When you believe you possess something as powerful and precious as God, what might you be willing to do to hold on to that preciousness and power? This is the danger of idolatry.

The mosque, the call to prayer, and the Qur'an are

not symbols I use to understand God. But for 1.5 billion people, they are powerful symbols pointing to that same reality. I cannot believe that my way is right and 1.5 billion people are wrong. Yes, some have claimed these symbols as their possessions and used them to legitimize violence, but their idolatry doesn't negate the sincere faith of so many others.

In my work as a chaplain, I continually teach and preach this very message. In a war zone, this job is all the more difficult and important because many of those who are trying to hurt and kill us claim to be Muslims. At this time in our history, all of us, soldiers and civilians, have a responsibility to respect the sincere faith of others, even when we disagree. Otherwise, we too practice idolatry. If we mistake our fingers for the moon, how are we theologically different from violent religious extremists?

There is a saying in my tradition by the sixteenth-century pastor and theologian Francis David: "We do not have to think alike to love alike." From this foundation, we can discover a God beyond mere symbols, a God who unites all people rather than being the cause of separation. Just as the light of the moon shines upon all people, so must the light of God illuminate all paths.

BURN BARREL WORSHIP

❖

It is a frigid night in Kandahar City. The tiny PSS has few amenities, consistent heat not among them. So as the time arrives for the evening worship service, we pull benches up to the burn barrel and sit close to keep warm. Smoke rises into the moonlit sky as the sounds of the third world echo just beyond the C-Wire and HESCOS.

There is no praise band, electric guitars, or drum kit; no PowerPoint or sound system; no pews, no stained glass, no stage or pulpit. I set up the same simple altar wherever I go, this time on a cigar box atop an over-turned barrel. No altar cloth or ornaments required.

Five or six gather close, all of us far from home, strangers in a strange land. Different ages, ethnicities, and faith backgrounds; some single, some married with kids, some unmarried with kids; from across the U.S.— yet all somehow the same. We gather in the name of one who long ago came to bring healing and hope to a broken world. Bread and wine pass among us. Prayers ancient and new are recited. How similar might it have been two thousand years ago as strangers and friends gathered in the cold and the dark seeking hope for a broken world?

In the flickering light of a burn barrel, Christ is present among us. It is not because we say the right words or have the right beliefs but because we share a common, ancient, and sacred hope that our brokenness will be made whole, that our fears will be quelled, and despite the reality of war, peace will be present among us for a few sacred moments.

So it has been in all times and places, wherever two or three are gathered, in every heart that shares in the hope of a world made new, the human and the divine live one life together. This is the great mystery of all true worship and the gift of one evening around a burn barrel.

TOWERS OF BABEL

———◆———

I have purchased a set of Islamic prayer beads from one of our local shop owners. The set has ninety-nine beads, one for each of the names of God in Islam. These are not literally God's names (as if we can call God Joe or Bob) but the attributes Muslims ascribe to the Holy, including the merciful, the shaper, the sustainer, the loving one.

In the biblical story of the Tower of Babel, the people hoped to reach God and "make their name famous" as if God were a thing to be used for their own vanity. As a result, the people of the world were scattered into diverse cultures and languages, presumably each with its own understanding of God.

In part, this reflects the pre-scientific worldview, in which God exists somewhere above us. The people thought they could stand face to face with God just by erecting a tall enough building. But the story is also about the human need to own and control things. When so much is out of our control, the lessons of Babel are important for all of us.

We can all build Towers of Babel when we use God for our own purposes. We can use God to dismiss others, to assert our superiority, to divide people into those who belong and those who don't. If we think God is a thing in a place, like the citizens of Babel did, we tend to decide that God is with "us" and not "them."

That is why I like the Islamic notion of ninety-nine names of God. Each of those names is a reminder that God is a reality woven into the very fabric of being. God cannot be named or held or possessed but must ultimately be experienced as love, justice, mercy, peace, compassion, creator, and more.

What names might you find for God? To put it another way, where have you experienced the Holy in your life, even here in this place? When does God feel far away? How has the divine been close to you? These questions can tear down the Towers of Babel in our minds and bring us down to earth, where God lives every day.

MEANING, PURPOSE AND EXPLOSIVES

———◆———

27 AUG 2011 PSS1 Kandahar City, Afghanistan. Young men and women go about their day. They're joking, sleeping, smoking, doing laundry, standing guard, like on any other day. Except for the AC that has just been fixed, there is nothing remarkable about this day. Make no mistake: This one simple comfort in an otherwise utterly uncomfortable place is reason enough to go on with the day. Sometimes that is all soldiers at war have.

Not far away, a man with a purpose gets behind the wheel of a Toyota SUV. His mind is numbed by drugs, but his purpose is sure. Someone somewhere has deluded him with a perverse and twisted view of the teachings of the Holy Qur'an. He has never heard the powerful message of justice woven through its pages. He has never been told of the Prophet's command never to harm the innocent. He knows only what he has been told: Drive the infidel from his land. Do the work Allah has commanded. Step up and do what is required to restore the righteous theocracy of the Taliban. He utterly and fully believes in his purpose. The meaning of his life has come to this.

Behind him in the SUV lie five hundred pounds of explosives. To you and me it seems so clear that such violence can have no place in any faith. To the vast majority of Muslims, many of whom I call friends, this man's beliefs are anathema. Nevertheless, he drives the muddy sewer-flooded road toward his goal with a firm belief that he is doing God's will.

Across the world, a young woman lies sleeping, dreaming of her beloved who will soon be home. A wedding must be planned. It will be small, in a courthouse, nothing fancy, but it is her dream. Right now it is her purpose, her meaning, to build a life with a young soldier. I can see her dreams like I saw my own so long ago: a home, a child to be the fulfillment of love's longing to be more than itself.

I cannot know what dreams the driver with the explosives had the night before. Such things are beyond my understanding. Did he dream of abandoning his family to be a faithful martyr? Did he dream of his god's delight in his glorious death? Did he have any questions of the justice of the path he was on? He was told, I am sure, to have no worries, that his family would be cared for. He was told to welcome death as a gift to God and the cause.

This is something difficult for the Western liberal mind to grasp, but it is vital that we try. We will never fully understand nor defeat this kind of extremism if we do not understand it. As much as we do not want to admit it, this kind of terrorism is religiously motivated. It is extremist and twisted, but still it is rooted in a religion. That religion happens to be Islam. It could be another. The fact that it is Islam cannot be allowed to cast a shadow upon the millions of Muslims who despise and denounce terrorism in every form. But the fact that there is a religious meaning and message behind it cannot be ignored. Living and working here under the constant threat of death at the hands of Islamic terrorists brings the power of religion to fuel evil into clear focus. Each day is a struggle to remember that the evil acts and perverted beliefs of so few cannot color the goodness of so many others.

Of course, we cannot blame religion alone. The young terrorist was fed a diet of theological hatred and lies. But it was he and no one else who ate so willingly at hatred's table. He chose his purpose. He made the choice to bring the meaning of his existence to this point. He is not tied to the SUV. The responsibility for the whole pointless exercise in death is his to bear. He chose the meaning of his life.

Life goes on inside the building. Guards in the tower scan their sectors for any sign of danger. Soldiers smoke their cigarettes. They think of home. They dream the dreams of young men and women throughout the ages. Leaders complete reports and prepare for the day to come.

The SUV rolls slowly through the mud. The thin metal gate is just yards from the road. From there, it is only several more yards to the flimsy low wall and the interior of the PSS. To the left stands the TOC. To the right are the sleeping bays. Between the two is a tiny courtyard. The interior of the TOC is all wood and metal. No concrete barriers. No HESCOs. No sandbags piled high. A large armored truck partially blocks the gate, but it's scant defense against five hundred pounds of HME.

The SUV turns and rams the thin metal gate. A young man turns at the noise. His mind races. The bomber rams again. The young soldier's mind puts the pieces together: explosives—friends—sleeping. In that moment, he forgets his love lying in bed at home. He forgets his wedding in just twelve days. He forgets his dreams. He forgets himself. All that exists in that moment are his friends. He runs toward them. They lie sleeping in the newly fixed AC. He forgets the thin metal gate that is just yards away. He forgets it all and runs and yells. He runs toward them, toward the gate. His meaning, his life's purpose in that moment, are one. So he forgets all else, even himself.

The bomber rams again. The gate, blocked by the armored truck, will not yield. But he will not be thwarted in his purpose. He detonates. Physics, not God, is now in control. A blast wave rolls forward. A tidal wave of uncontrolled force at twice the speed of sound hurtles forth. It crumples everything before it: the SUV, the thin metal gate, the armored truck, the bomber. They all become shrapnel propelled by fanatical hate.

Across the world, the young woman sleeps on, unaware of the meaning of any of this. Her dreams remain untouched. Her hopes are intact. Her love for him is as real as ever. In the morning she will wake to a new world. She will have to fill that new world with new meaning and new purpose. Will it be any more or less a world than before? Will her new dreams be any less? Will her new hopes be diminished or enlarged? Does any of this matter? Is there any more meaning or purpose in her life, or her fiancé's, or the bomber's? Are these meanings equal? Who chooses such things? Who is to say what the point is?

The young soldier turns. The gate hurtles toward him, now a ball of burning hot, knife-sharp steel. Does he see it? Does he know his friends will be safe? The gate slices through his head. Without another thought, without another breath, a young soldier is dead.

MEANING IN THE MIDST OF WAR

◆

"Bison Main, this is Dark Horse 6-1, show SP Camp Nathan Smith, 4 victors, 19 pax have the chaplain and we are en route to PSS1."

"Dark Horse 1-6, be aware possible IED on your route vicinity of the Kandahar University. Be advised that air is RED no medivac birds available."

"Roger Bison Main, 1-6 out."

I rumble down the street in the back of an MATV, a smaller more maneuverable version of the Mine Resistant Ambush Protected truck. Piped into my headset is a soldier's "combat mix," a surreal mix of death metal and Southern fried rock. The convoy commander, twenty-three-year-old Sergeant Barley, navigates the four vehicles (victors) and nineteen passengers (pax) through the ancient, crowded, and dangerous streets of Kandahar City, Afghanistan. There have been several IEDs found across the city in the past seventy-two hours. With vigilance and luck, all were found before they detonated. Still we are prepared, every time we go out, to get blown up. Most of the time when this hap-

pens, the truck is mine-resistant enough to save lives . . .
most of the time. This is the backdrop against which I
conduct my ministry every day.

I am headed to Police Sub Station 1 (PSS1). Just
weeks before, a suicide bomber attacked this PSS, kill-
ing a young soldier and wounding five others. I arrived
forty-five minutes after the blast and helped the remain-
der of the platoon clean up the debris and begin put-
ting their lives back together. I prayed over the mangled
body of the soldier before he began his long trip home.
I helped mop up blood from the floors and walls. I literally dug in and did the hard work of combat ministry.
This was not the first dead soldier I have sent home. He
was not the last. I am acutely aware that before I step
foot on American soil again, there will be more.

As an Army chaplain, my job is to help young men
and women make sense out of all this. But there are
times I cannot make sense of it myself. In this place, exis-
tential questions are not philosophy discussed at coffee
hour. While every human being must struggle with what
it means to be human and thus to be mortal, zipping a
black bag over the breathless body of a friend puts a new
sense of urgency on the questions of life and death.

That is one of the reasons I am here, why I became
an Army chaplain, and why I rumble down the crowded
and dangerous streets of Kandahar City nearly every
day. As a Unitarian Universalist, I understand there are
no easy answers. Instead, I seek to engage the young

men and women I meet in the struggle for human meaning. Many chaplains do not share this approach to ministry. They offer the easy answers. They imagine a deity that has charted each of our courses in life from our first breath to our last. I cannot share this point of view. If this is true, has God placed some of us on a collision course with an IED? Some tell soldiers to pray the sinner's prayer and never fear death again. If your friend never said these words, should you fear for him?

Easy answers lead to difficult questions. So why not just start with the questions?

As time goes on in a combat zone, the questions don't slow down and the answers don't get easier. Far from home with the threat of violence looming beneath the surface of life, how one reconciles the message of Jesus with the reality of war comes into acute focus. It's not as easy as original sin or God's mysterious plan. I am thankful it is not, and I am grateful to be here as a constant reminder of that truth.

I have never believed in a predetermined "plan of salvation" in which Jesus and all the rest of us are no more than pawns. Jesus was born in the perfectly normal way all human beings are born to perfectly normal parents. The angels, the magi, and the star in the sky came long afterward to establish the significance of the life of Jesus in light of his death. So why the stories? Those who knew him saw something powerful, something ultimately real about him. They struggled to make sense of his tragic and violent death through the symbols and stories of their times.

Here in combat, we too are engaged in the same struggle to find meaning in a world of violence and uncertainty. The simple fix—pray the sinner's prayer, accept Jesus, and walk away—might be an easier way to deal with it all, but the questions of being and nothingness remain and will eat away at the edges of your spirit. No matter how you choose to run and hide from the reality of war, it will keep coming at you until you recognize that you are the only person who can give meaning to your own life.

If angels, magi, and roving stars did not accompany the birth of Jesus, then meaning lies not in a miraculous birth but in an exceptional life—a life that ended in betrayal, injustice, and violence. The birth, and therefore the life of Jesus, must remind us that, far from being complete, our lives and our world are fragmented and imperfect. Jesus saw this imperfect world and imperfect human beings not as utterly fallen, beyond redemption, or requiring the intervention of an otherworldly deity to make us into something we are not. He saw the world—*just as it was and is*—as God's world. He saw human beings—*just as we are*—as God's people. What mattered to him was how we respond to God's imperfect world and God's imperfect people.

Jesus taught us to respond to violence by turning the other cheek. He taught us to love thy neighbor as thyself. What happens when your "neighbor" is trying to kill you? You cannot turn the other cheek when you have a split-second to "take the shot" that may save your buddies' lives. If you fire, how do you deal with the knowledge that you took the life of another human being? These questions are not your typical coffee hour discussion but issues I face on a regular basis. I can tell you that easy answers don't cut it.

Thrown into this broken world, dreadful circumstances sometimes require us to do awful things. When this happens, the life of Christ requires that we turn to each other and see God's people. The life of Christ beckons us to meet our fragmented selves with compassion—standing with, walking with, hoping with, and loving with our fellow human beings.

I believe, I hope, and I pray that I do these things every day, yet I cannot tell you how to do them. I cannot reach into my pocket and pull out my leather-bound red-letter edition of the Soldier's Bible and point to the answer. In combat, honesty demands that we finally come clean with ourselves and admit that answers do not exist, only questions and only human responses to human frailty.

"Praetorian Base, this is Dark Horse 1-6. We are RP PSS1. 4 Victors, 18 Pax. We've got the chaplain for you."

"Roger, 6-1. Send him in."

"Already on his way, see you next time. 1-6 out."

I haul myself up the dusty entry road and into the now cleaned up PSS. Dropping my gear, I look around at the scene. A new building stands there now, where debris and death were not so long ago. A young soldier sees me from a distance and quickens his step to greet me. I have not seen him since I sent his friend on his final ride home. He throws his arms around me; the embrace nearly takes my breath away with its power.

"Sir, I'm so glad you're here. We missed you," he says, with his arms still tight around me.

In that single moment, all my questions, all my fears, all my confusion faded away. I knew why I was here, why I do what I do, and what it means to live in a broken and fragmented world. There is nothing in the world I would have rather done that day than rumble down the dirty, ancient, dangerous streets of Kandahar City, building meaning in the midst of war.

TRIP WIRES AND FORTS

◆

Our mission here is to partner with local police and assist them in the task of maintaining security in the region. U.S. soldiers live and work side by side with Afghan national policemen in small compounds called PSSs. Some PSSs share walls with local villages, making security an issue. It would not be difficult nor unusual for an insurgent to climb over a wall with no good intent. I walk into one PSS that shares such a wall. It is hard not to notice the soda cans hanging from the concertina wire. It is Christmas, so I imagine the cans are field-expedient decorations. I ask an NCO, "What's with the cans?" He reaches up and shakes a can. It rattles. It is filled with stones. "Lieutenant had us put them up. Field-expedient warning system." We both smile as I shake the warning cans.

It reminds me of the fort I built as a kid with my friends Marc and Clint. We surrounded the area with trip-wires and hung tin cans, bottles, and other junk to warn us if the enemy was near. In the fort, anything was possible. We lived in an open world.

We still live in an open world, though it can be hard to see it. That means it's wise to be prepared for anything. But it also means we're not just along for the ride. We are participants in creation. The world is not complete and each of us has a part to play in the ongoing story of creation.

Some say creation happened long ago and was over in six days, that the future is predestined. Some say that virtue is following the path rather than resisting the predetermined direction.

If we believe that creation is ongoing, we are each responsible not just for our actions but for the kind of world we live in. If the world is not what we hope for, it is our responsibility to change it.

What kind of world do you want to live in? We can live in a world of anger, fear, and vengeance or a world of hope and compassion. In a combat zone, this dichotomy is strikingly clear. In one moment, all is calm, almost peaceful, but in a second, with no more warning than rattling stones in a soda can, all can be deadly confusion. Here I have felt this truth more fully than I imagined possible. But I wonder how or if I will take it with me. It is not an experience I want to forget. Knowing the fragility of peace in such a real way gives those who have served in war insights rarely understood by others.

Even if you've never had to experience the violence of war, you can probably think of a time when your heart has turned to a kind of destructive inner violence. Those moments when a misspoken word or something left unsaid has spun you into a kind of deadly confusion. Soldiers or civilians, we all fight battles.

A SOLDIER'S BURDEN

———◆———

Jesus said, "Come unto me, all ye that labor and are heavy laden, and I will give you rest. Take my yoke upon you, and learn of me . . . and ye shall find rest unto your souls. For my yoke is easy, and my burden is light."

The most important word here may be *of*. Jesus wanted people to learn *of* him, not *from* him, or even *about* him. He wanted people to know him and how he lived. The people Jesus was talking to were already burdened. They were those in society who worked so that that the rich and powerful would not have to. Imagine what the image "take my yoke upon you" would evoke in the agricultural society that Jesus lived in. It describes working and getting your hands dirty, sweating and doing hard labor. It must have been startling to hear. I can imagine Jesus preaching this message at the end of a long hard day to a group of hot tired laborers. What might they have thought? "You kidding me, Jesus? One more burden? A yoke? Do you know how hard it is already?"

Yet Jesus knew that true freedom requires taking on something that matters in life, something that has weight, a burden in the sense that you have to carry it with you everywhere you go. But paradoxically, if you do that, you will find rest. Your life will become more meaningful, powerful, and free.

Living and working in combat—knowing that just outside the gate are people who would like to kill you, seeing your friends shot dead or blown to bits before your eyes—makes it is easy to become hateful and angry. For us, the more difficult way, the yoke Jesus spoke of, is to face the violence, the danger, the pain, and the anger of war as he did, without embarking on revenge or building hate in our hearts. This is how we are called to live our lives.

Saying this is simple. Doing it is very difficult. But as theologian Howard Thurman said, "Jesus rejected hatred . . . because he saw that hatred meant death to the mind, death to the spirit, death to communion with his Father. He affirmed life; and hatred was the great denial." In the face of so much death, we must turn to each other in compassion and caring and affirm that God's love is more powerful than our deepest hatred and most burning anger. Only then will our yoke be easy and our burden light.

THE COURAGE TO CARE

◆

The earliest human creation myths include references to the need for human companionship. In Genesis we read, "Then the Lord God said, 'It is not good that the man should be alone.'" From our earliest beginnings, humanity has recognized that we need one another.

There is a kind of courage we often forget and don't give ourselves credit for. I call it the courage to care. It takes a certain kind of strength to overcome the fear we might face on a dismounted patrol or confirming an IED. But for many, these fears are things we just put out of our minds. As I drive around Kandahar City, I rarely give a thought to the IED threat or the latest report of a VBIED. These things just fade into the background.

Living in a combat zone, knowing the real danger we all face and caring about and for others takes real courage. We live and work with each other 24/7, we get close to each other, we hear about each other's kids, wives, husbands, and friends—all with the specter of the next IED or spectacular attack looming over us.

After losing a friend this deployment, I have wondered if it is worth the risk, the work, and the pain to get to know anyone else. Would it be easier to just scrape the surface and not get so close that I will be forced to care for someone again? I am not alone in these feelings.

But the cost of not caring is far higher than the pain or grief of loss. When we cut ourselves off from others out of fear, we forfeit our humanity to that fear. This is the essence of real courage, the willingness to risk loss in order to achieve a greater good. We discover our full humanity by being related, connected to others. Without real relationship and meaningful connection we cannot become our true selves. When we avoid connection in an attempt to avoid the pain of loss what are we really giving up?

Caring demands an investment of our time, energy, and emotions. Ultimately, caring is a dangerous proposition. Your caring may not be returned. Your willingness to risk may not be understood. Others who fear being hurt may seek to avoid connection and reject your efforts. Someone you have grown to care for may die.

When you choose to care, you tell the world that despite all these risks, there is some truth larger than ourselves that makes every loss, every grief, and every disappointment worth the risk. I can't explain how or why this happens. But I have experienced this truth beyond hows and whys.

When things just don't seem to make sense, our caring gives meaning to our lives. Sometimes when nothing makes sense, all we can do is care and that very act itself brings meaning. So it is that the courage to care may be the greatest courage we can display.

BLESSED LITTLE GIRL

—◆—

I hear a group of soldiers laughing as they recall a motorcycle accident that sent a little girl flying over a rickshaw. "Did you see how she flew? She must have gone twenty feet! Amazing. It was like *Jack-Ass*." I hear those words and laughter and imagine a similar scene could have taken place two thousand years ago as Jesus spoke his blessings and Roman Centurions laughed at those Jesus was there to bless.

Jesus said, "Blessed are the poor; Blessed are the reviled; Blessed are those who weep; Blessed are the hungry; Blessed is the one who has suffered." Jesus challenged a system of division and blame that assured wealth and power stayed in the hands of a very few. The reviled and outcast were dehumanized to keep an out-of-balance system from toppling under the weight of its own injustice. Jesus upset the balance by humanizing those whom others saw as less than human.

Most of us would not consider ourselves to be wealthy or powerful. Yet in some ways, here in Kandahar, we are. We have the weapons. We have the money.

63

We have much of the power. As warriors, we sometimes think we must dehumanize others to carry out our often violent missions. But I believe that, as warriors, we must do all we can to avoid dehumanization. If we look at others as less than persons, what does that do to us? Do we really want to be the kind of people that laugh at little girls getting hurt? Dehumanizing others allows Al-Qaeda, the Taliban, and others to target indiscriminately those they revile. We cannot become like them.

Jesus recognized, I believe in a unique way, that all people are blessed. What does this mean for all of us? How must we use our power? How must we look at those who are just trying to live their lives in this broken world where so many suffer?

It may be as simple as this: Don't laugh. Stop and help.

A STONE'S THROW

◆

As I ride through Kandahar City's Sub-District 9, I see a naked dust-covered kid playing along the road. That is not the strangest thing. But when he picks up a large rock and hurls it at the truck, I wonder aloud, "What the hell? Who lets their kid run around naked throwing rocks? What kind of place is this?"

Years of war and violence have produced a perversely unique system, where hurling rocks at others is a legitimate sport. It is easy to become cynical, even contemptuous, of those kids who throw rocks. However, we must not allow our anger to numb our compassion. In a place like this, compassion for a dirty rock-throwing kid is all that keeps us human.

If our entire world, from our first breaths, was a closely circumscribed existence defined by poverty, war, death, dirt, and dust, how would we perceive the world around us? How different would we be? Maybe rock throwing would not seem so strange.

My son has grown up seeing men in uniform as "the good guys," not a threat. When his bunny rabbit died, he cried for a day and buried it in the back yard. That is as close to death as he has ever been. He takes a hot bath every night. He has ice-cold water, juice, and soda for the taking. His world is secure, reliable, and good. He is happy, safe, and loved.

That kid with the rock has never known the world my son takes for granted. His world is not secure, reliable, and good. It is dangerous, uncertain, and rough. Still, he knows how to throw rocks. It is one certain thing in an uncertain world. So that is what he does. Understanding this, my response is compassion, compassion for a child who seeks to hurt me, compassion for a child who is no less a child of God than my own son.

I cannot change his world, but I can—I *must*—try to understand it. Otherwise, a kid with a rock is just one more kind of enemy instead of the person he really is, a kid who, like my own son, only wants to be happy, safe, and loved.

GRAVES AND PLAYGROUNDS

◆

There's a playground in Kandahar that sits in the middle of a Taliban graveyard. It's a center of activity for area kids. I have watched as kids no older than five or six engaged in knock-down, drag-out, rock-throwing fights among the graves over swing sets and sliding boards. Yet another WTF moment in Afghanistan.

I know so little about a world where kids learn to fight before they can read and where graves sit next to teeter-totters. This reveals a truth about war that humbles even the strongest among us. We're humbled not so much by fear as by the knowledge of our own mortality, and even more by the realization of how little we know at all.

I could become superior and self-inflated at how much more civilized *we* are than *them*. That would be the easy way to rationalize what I don't comprehend and thus avoid the powerful questions of justice inherent in graves next to playgrounds. In the end, when I am really being honest with myself, humility is the response that feels right.

If humility is the heart's truthful response to unknowing, pride and superiority are ways to defend against the painful truth we witness in war. I do not understand why the world is so unfair, why my child is safe and an Afghan child is not. If I tell myself it is because *we* are better than *them*, the world makes sense. When there is a good reason an Afghan kid must play in a graveyard and fight for a swing, I can remain safely entombed in my self-imposed ignorance.

But if I am humble, I can admit there is never any good reason for the suffering of a child. I can honestly say that the world does not always make sense. I can face the truth that whatever meaning there is in war depends on my response to suffering, injustice, and pain.

Right now, I am not sure how to make sense of graves and playgrounds. But at least I am able to admit my unknowing. If this world is ever to makes sense, if there is any meaning to be coaxed from the absurdity of it all, it will begin in humility.

A BEAR AND A BUNNY

---◆---

As I walk through a crowded street, I spot a little boy holding two familiar objects. This time they are not stones but a stuffed bear and a stuffed bunny. I kneel down and hold my hand out to him. He smiles and runs away. Moments later, he returns, bear and bunny in hand. I reach for the bunny, which I discover he holds with a grip that refuses to give.

The animals he holds are clearly high-quality. I imagine they arrived in some care package somewhere. Both the animals and the child stand out on the street. His smile too is impossible to miss. When I see him, I cannot help but smile myself. It is not until later, when I look at the photo I took, that the most interesting thing appears to me: The animals are still nearly completely white.

I almost don't believe it. I enlarge the picture for a closer look. It confirms what I have suspected. There is hardly a mark or stain anywhere. The boy's clothes are as dirty as any other kid's. His face is in need of a wash. But the bear and bunny remain nearly snow white.

These two simple toys are that child's most prized possessions. I can only imagine how much care it must take to keep them clean in the streets of Kandahar, where everything is dirty. When you have so little, these simple things, things most of us take for granted, mean so much.

Imagine if you will that your most treasured possession is a stuffed bear or bunny. Imagine that the thing that brings you joy, security, and contentment is something so simple.

Sometimes it takes a child to remind us that our most prized possession is in our arms, even when we cannot see it because of what we think we must have. When Jesus said, "Let the little children come to me, and do not stop them; for it is to such as these that the kingdom of heaven belongs," he was talking about children just like the little boy with a bear and a bunny, who are happy just as they are.

May each of us be so blessed in our own lives.

THE BACKSPACE KEY

My computer, the one I am writing on now, has lost the backspace key. It was loose for a while. Then it began to fall off, but I could usually reattach it. Then one day, I came back to my office and it was gone. Now there is just an empty space and a few metal connectors where it used to be.

Amazingly, I can still backspace. I just need to think carefully about it and press in just the right spot. It does make me more careful in my typing; I have to think more about what I am going back to erase. I suppose many things in life are like that, things we should think carefully about before we try to redo them. Some things can't be redone at all.

As I think about why that key was the first to go, I realize that I was probably using it too much and pressing it too hard. That too is something to think about. I probably need to be less concerned about what is to the left of the cursor and think more about what is about to appear to the right.

How will what I do now affect others and myself in

71

the future? In the military, we call this idea *second- and third-order effects*. Everything we do has effects, some we can anticipate and some we cannot. Buddhists call this *pratītyasamutpāda* or interdependent co-arising. The Buddha explained it by saying, "This is, because that is. This is not, because that is not. This comes to be, because that comes to be. This ceases to be, because that ceases to be."

More simply put, what we do matters because it will always affect something or someone else. If we spend all our time worrying about what we have done, we may not pay enough attention to what we are doing in the present. In life, we can't just hit the backspace key and retype.

FORGIVENESS IS HUMAN

◆

The moon rises as the call to prayer begins to ring out over the city. I stop for just a moment to take in the view. The end of our deployment is finally in sight. "Two more full moons in Kandahar," I think. So much has happened in such a short time. How we each look back upon our experiences, in large part, will determine their meaning to us in the years to come.

Mistakes. What ifs. If onlys. We can easily fill our minds with an unceasing train of thoughts about how things might have been. In the military, this human tendency to over-analyze our errors is compounded by an institutional culture in which we are often "only as good as our last mistake."

At its root, the word *forgiveness* means to give up or to give away. When you forgive, you give away your power to punish or take retribution. When you forgive, you let go of something, you give up something, a weight is released from your shoulders.

We often think about forgiveness as releasing another person from an obligation to us, from responsi-

73

bility for their actions. In truth, through forgiveness, we free ourselves. We free ourselves from the desire to take revenge, the need to get even, and from anger. Without forgiveness, we carry these weights with us wherever we go. With forgiveness, we can put down these burdens.

This is why self-forgiveness may be the most important kind of forgiveness we engage in. When we fail to forgive ourselves, we are forced to carry a double burden—punishing ourselves with nagging questions and self-doubt, plus guilt and shame over knowing we could have done better.

It's easy to look back on deployment or any important phase of our lives and wonder what we could have or should have done differently. We can second-guess our best choices for a lifetime and become trapped in a debilitating cycle of self-doubt.

In truth, the most important question to ask is how we will learn from and live with the choices we have made. There are thousands of things we could have done differently, but there is only one way to move on: forgive ourselves for our shortcomings and commit to doing better in the days to come. We don't have to give our memories over to regret. Alexander Pope said, "To err is human. To forgive is divine." But sometimes forgiveness is the most human thing we can do—not just for others, but for ourselves as well.

WAIT AND HOPE

———◆———

Buddhists see patience as a virtue to be perfected in order to obtain enlightenment. Many Muslims undertake a discipline of patience in order to grow closer to Allah. In Judaism, the book of Job is in many ways a long reflection on patience in the face of suffering. Waiting in patience is a central theme found in the history of Christianity.

Soldiers in combat and at home spend a lot of time waiting. Anyone who has spent even a moment in the military knows the phrase "hurry up and wait." The second half of deployment, particularly, is a severe challenge to patience. Sometimes the closer we get to something, the harder it is to wait. The desired event feels more real to us as time passes and our longing for it becomes more palpable. The waiting becomes painful. We fear it will never end.

That is why we must wait with hope. To wait with hope is the religious meaning of patience. Hope reminds us that we are not just marking time but moving toward something meaningful, toward the people and things that really matter to us. Hope is a faith in the future, joyful anticipation of what can be rather than mourning what we do not yet have.

PACKING LISTS

It's time to start thinking about what I will bring home from Afghanistan. The Army has given us a list of the things we can and cannot take with us. I have spent several nights war-gaming how I will pack, what I will mail, and what I will stash away in a shipping container that will eventually reach home station.

The fact that we can now really start to think about these things and that we have seen some stuff get packed, inspected, and sealed up for shipping is a great reminder that our time is getting short. It has led me to think about how, over the past year, we have each accumulated varying amounts of baggage. Some of it we can leave behind. Some we will have to carry with us, whether we want to or not.

We often make the mistake of thinking that everything we pack is our own choice. We believe that if an experience or memory is one we would rather not deal with, we can just leave it behind. The truth is that many of the things we have done and experienced here will remain with us for the rest of our lives, and we don't always get to choose.

Yet despite what we see on the evening news, we needn't be haunted by memories of war. Everything we have experienced can become part of who we are and bring deeper meaning and purpose to our lives.

I will not complete this deployment without carrying fears, loneliness, regrets, grief, and pain away with me. I have had these experiences. There is no way I can ignore or forget these things. Yet these things needn't be harmful or depressing. I do not have to believe they make me less than I am or that they will become lingering memories rather than strengths.

Our emotional packing list is not made up of the things we will leave behind so much as those we will bring home. It's not about hiding these memories away but learning to integrate our experiences into who we will become. My fear has taught me to understand the fear of others. My regret has taught me to forgive as I would be forgiven. My grief has taught me to savor every precious moment of life. My loneliness has taught me to cultivate friendship. My pain has taught me the power of compassion.

The experience of being human, though sometimes difficult and painful, remains filled with possibility.

RETURN

◆

The first stop on U.S. soil after a deployment is the airport. From there, it's all downhill until you get to see your family and loved ones again. But the airport is its own scene when you're a soldier in uniform.

On my trip home, I'm reminded of the last time I was in the airport—returning from Afghanistan after two weeks of "R and R," or Rest and Relaxation leave.

In my memory I walk through the crowded Atlanta Airport. I am tired and feeling sorry for myself. I certainly do not want to shake hands and play the happy, grateful soldier one more time. I have to admit that I have become weary of the "thank you for your service" handshakes. I understand the sentiment and appreciate the gesture, but sometimes you just really need to get to the bathroom. When I see the group of elementary school students holding signs and clapping, my heart sinks. I need to go, not shake hands, but there seems no good way to avoid it; they have chosen the only clear path to the restroom to set up the greeting line.

I make a wide arc and head for my destination. Then from out of the crowd, a kindly-looking older lady in a USO shirt yells to me, "Sir, could you please come and talk to them, just a few words? It would mean so much!" All eyes are suddenly on me. I can't avoid them now. My name is clearly emblazoned on my chest. I can see the headline, "Chaplain Tyger, U.S. Army, Runs Away from Children in Display of Ingratitude." I turn and walk toward them.

"Hi guys. Where are you from? What are your names? What brings you out today?" I smile and do my duty.

"We just want to say thanks," one student says. "We really appreciate your sacrifice."

Frankly, I have never considered my service a sacrifice. I am well paid to do this job and I really love what I do, two things many people in this world cannot say. Privilege? Yes. Honor? Certainly. But sacrifice? It just doesn't feel that way to me.

Nonetheless, I wade into the crowd of kids and make some of the typical small talk soldiers make in these situations. I share little pieces of information but never allow anything like a real conversation to develop. I guess there are some things only other soldiers will understand. The real sacrifices we make—the sorrow, the fear, the loneliness, the questions that will remain forever unanswered—these are not things we share in airports.

As I talk with the kids, I give my usual "I'm just a soldier" speech. I've recited it to many strangers in many airports. I tell them how much it means for them to come out to thank us and how important it is for us to hear that they appreciate our "sacrifice."

I look at their faces as they gather in close, shake my hand, and ask their questions with wide-eyed curiosity. That is when something strange happens. I begin to feel my voice crack. A lump forms in my throat. My eyes feel strangely wet. The words become difficult to get out of my mouth. I really need to get myself out of there fast before I break down.

"Well, thanks guys. I really gotta go. . . ." are the only words I manage to squeak out as I turn and walk away.

Something about that encounter gets to me. Maybe it is that those kids remind me of my own. Maybe it is the genuineness of their appreciation or the way they seem to look up to me just because I wear a uniform. There is nothing special about me. I am just a guy lucky enough to wear a uniform and do a job I love. But for a moment, a fleeting moment, I feel truly appreciated for what I do in a more genuine way than I have ever felt before. That appreciation means something.

As I walk out of the bathroom, I think of all the big geopolitical issues I heard on the news at home. I think of the political pundits making ill-informed judgments about the "value of the mission," "the chances of success," and even "the ultimate meaning of soldiers' sacrifices" (like they could really know about such things).

Looking in those kids' eyes, all those questions vanished as I recognized a very simple truth: What we do matters. Whatever historians may write or pundits pontificate, what we do matters because we stand for more than any single mission, geopolitical strategy, or political goal.

Honor, devotion, loyalty, friendship, and yes, sacrifice have meaning and value far beyond what any TV talking head or politician may say in the moment. I think it was these values—which we have all, in some way, dedicated our lives to—that I saw in those kids' eyes and that nearly brought me to tears (not an easy thing to do).

Now as I walk through an airport in uniform and I am greeted with "thank you for your service," I can read more into what is being said. Maybe the uniform we wear reminds people that the sacrifices we make every day and will bear the rest of our lives, we make not for ourselves, and not for them, but for something greater than any of us may ever truly know or understand. Maybe they are saying, "Thank you for reminding us that, despite all the BS and confusion of life, there remain some truths that are truly worth fighting for."

MILITARY TERMS

◆

11B Infantryman   Member of the Military Occupational Specialty 11B, the main land combat force in the Army. The Infantryman's role is to be ready to defend our country in peacetime and to capture, destroy, and repel enemy ground forces during combat.

ACU   Army Combat Uniform. The familiar digital camouflage pattern uniform worn by members of the U.S. Army.

AUP   Afghan Uniformed Police. A broad term referring to a variety of uniformed police personnel, distinct from the Afghan National Army. During my year in Afghanistan we worked primarily with the Afghan National Police.

Burn Pit   A pit in a military base where the daily trash and waste is disposed of, since there is little to no sanitation system in Afghanistan.

Deployment   Any long-term movement of a military unit from its home station to a particular area of operation. In this book, *deployment* refers to a combat deployment, in which soldiers are sent from home to a combat zone.

The Field An overnight or longer training event while at home. Soldiers "go to the field" any time we train away from home for more than one day.

HESCO The brand name for a collapsible wire mesh container with a heavy-duty fabric liner, used as a barrier against blasts or small arms. HESCOs are set up, then filled with dirt or sand to create heavy-duty barriers capable of stopping blasts.

Hooah A term used throughout the Army that indicates all the coolest, hardcore jobs. It can also be used almost any time and any place to mean anything, except no.

IED Improvised Explosive Device. IEDs may be made from a vast array of materials, from unexploded ordnance used in previous conflicts to fertilizer and fuel oil. They may be hidden underground, in culverts, in vehicles, or in vests worn by insurgents. These devices could be hiding anywhere and are one of the primary weapons used by insurgents.

Insurgent The anti-Afghan forces fighting to subvert the legitimate Afghan government.

MATV Mine Resistant All-Terrain Vehicle. A large,

heavily armored truck built on a dump truck frame, the MATV could resist small arms fire, IEDs, and rocket-propelled grenades. It served as my primary means of transportation in Afghanistan.

Mission   Nearly any assignment, from the overall mission of defeating terrorism to an individual unit's mission to secure an area. My mission in Afghanistan was to care for the spiritual needs of soldiers. That included many smaller missions, such as visiting soldiers, conducting religious services, and sometimes just being present.

Multicam   The standard, non-digital camouflage pattern used in Afghanistan. This pattern performs better than the Army Combat Uniform in the rugged Afghan terrain.

NCO   Non-Commissioned Officer. An enlisted soldier with the rank of Corporal, Sergeant, Staff Sergeant, Sergeant First Class, Master Sergeant, or Sergeant Major. The primary on-the-ground leaders of soldiers, NCOs are referred to as the backbone of the Army.

PSS   Police Sub Station. A local police station where Afghan Uniformed Police and U.S. forces live and work together to bring basic security to an area.

Stateside   Home, the United States of America.

Sub-District   In Afghanistan each province is divided into districts. Each district is divided into sub-districts. These sub-districts are similar to a neighborhood one might find in the United States. For instance, Soho in Manhattan, which is a part of New York City, which is part of New York State.

TOC   Tactical Operations Center. The nerve center of combat operations where all activity is tracked.

Trip Wire   A wire or string often connected to an explosive device. It could also be connected to some form of early warning device.

USO   United Service Organization. A non-profit, non-governmental organization dedicated to supporting U.S. troops around the world. In Afghanistan the USO provides this support through small movie theaters, video gaming facilities, and general rest and relaxation facilities.

VBIED   Vehicle Born Improvised Explosive Device. Basically a car bomb, it can be remotely detonated or driven by a suicide bomber.

If you enjoyed this book, you might also like

Bless All Who Serve

Sources of Hope, Courage and Faith for Military
Personnel and Their Families

edited by Matthew and Gail Tittle
(Skinner House Books, 2010)

A pocket-sized and durable little book of readings and
songs from many faith traditions, ancient and modern,
plus reflections by veterans and military chaplains.
Speaks to themes of commitment, courage, patriotism, freedom, strength and service. Reflection topics
include fear of injury and death, grief, peace and violence, hope and despair, separation from loved ones
and honoring the fallen.

Available at the Unitarian Universalist Association
Bookstore (www.uuabookstore.org, 1-800-215-9076)
and bookstores everywhere. Also sold as an eBook
through the Amazon Kindle store and Google Play.

Free copies of Bless All Who Serve are available to military chaplains, ministers, and men and women of all
faiths who are in the service. Chaplains and ministers
should contact Julie Shaw (mplassistant@uua.org) at
the UUA. Servicemen and women should contact Lorraine Dennis (ldennis@clfuu.org) at the Church of the
Larger Fellowship.